let's cook

mexican

Marlena
Spieler

p

Refried Bean Nachos

*A Mexican classic, refried beans and tortilla crisps are topped
with luscious melted cheese, salsa, and assorted toppings, to make an irresistible dip.
Perfect for an informal gathering!*

Serves 6–8

INGREDIENTS

400 g/14 oz refried beans
400 g/14 oz can pinto beans, drained
large pinch of ground cumin
large pinch of mild chilli powder
175 g/6 oz bag tortilla chips

225 g/8 oz grated cheese, such as
 Cheddar
salsa of your choice
1 avocado, stoned (pitted), diced
 and tossed with lime juice
½ small onion or 3–5 spring onions
 (scallions), chopped

2 ripe tomatoes, diced
handful of shredded lettuce
3–4 tbsp chopped fresh coriander
 (cilantro)
soured cream, to serve

1 Place the refried beans in a pan with the pinto beans, cumin and chilli powder. Add enough water to make a thick soup-like consistency, stirring gently so that the beans do not lose their texture.

2 Heat the bean mixture over a medium heat until hot, then reduce the heat and keep the mixture warm while you prepare the rest of the dish.

3 Arrange half the tortilla chips in the bottom of a flameproof casserole or gratin dish and cover with the bean mixture. Sprinkle with the cheese and bake in a preheated oven at 200°C/400°F/ Gas Mark 6 until the cheese melts.

4 Alternatively, place the casserole under the grill (broiler) and grill (broil) for 5–7 minutes or until the cheese melts and lightly sizzles in places.

5 Arrange on top of the melted cheese the salsa, avocado, onion, tomato, lettuce and fresh coriander (cilantro). Surround with the remaining tortilla chips and serve immediately with with soured cream.

VARIATION

Replace the soured cream with Greek yogurt as an alternative.

Hot Tomato Sauce

This tangy sauce is excellent with crispy tortillas and tostadas, or with grilled (broiled) or fried fish. Try it with fish and chips for a change!

Serves 4

INGREDIENTS

2–3 fresh green chillies, such as
   jalapeño or serrano
225 g/8 oz canned chopped
   tomatoes
1 spring onion (scallion), thinly
   sliced

2 garlic cloves, chopped
2–3 tbsp cider vinegar
50–80 ml/2–3 fl oz/$^1/_4$–$^1/_3$
   cup water
large pinch of dried oregano
large pinch of ground cumin

large pinch of sugar
large pinch of salt

1 Slice the chillies open,
remove the seeds if wished,
then chop the chillies.

2 Put the chillies in a blender
or food processor together
with the tomatoes, spring onion
(scallion), garlic, vinegar, water,
oregano, cumin, sugar and salt.
Process until smooth.

3 Adjust the seasoning and chill
until ready to serve. The
sauce will keep for up to a week,
covered, in the refrigerator.

COOK'S TIP

*If you have sensitive skin, it may
be advisable to wear rubber gloves
when preparing chillies, as the oil
in the seeds and flesh can cause
irritation. Make sure that you do
not touch your eyes when handling
cut chillies.*

Two Classic Salsas

A Mexican meal is not complete without an accompanying salsa. These two traditional salsas are ideal for seasoning any dish, from filled tortillas to grilled (broiled) meat – they add a spicy hotness that is the very essence of Mexican cooking.

Serves 4–6

INGREDIENTS

JALAPEÑO SALSA:
1 onion, finely chopped
2–3 garlic cloves, finely chopped
4–6 tbsp coarsely chopped pickled
    jalapeño chillies
juice of ½ lemon
about ¼ tsp ground cumin
salt

SALSA CRUDA:
6–8 ripe tomatoes, finely chopped
about 100 ml/3½ fl oz/scant ½ cup
    tomato juice
3–4 garlic cloves, finely chopped
½–1 bunch fresh coriander (cilantro)
    leaves, coarsely chopped
pinch of sugar

3–4 fresh green chillies, such as
    jalapeño or serrano, deseeded
    and finely chopped
½–1 tsp ground cumin
3–4 spring onions (scallions), finely
    chopped
salt

1 To make the jalapeño salsa, put the onion in a bowl with the garlic, jalapeños, lemon juice and cumin. Season with salt and stir together. Cover and chill until required.

2 To make a chunky-textured salsa cruda, stir all the ingredients together in a bowl, adding salt to taste. Cover and chill until required.

3 To make a smoother-textured salsa, process the ingredients in a blender or food processor. Cover and chill until required.

VARIATION

For the salsa cruda, substitute finely chopped orange segments and deseeded diced cucumber for the tomatoes to add a fresh, fruity taste.

COOK'S TIP

You can vary the amount of garlic, chillies and ground spices according to taste, but make sure the salsa has quite a 'kick', otherwise it will not be effective.

Santa Fe
Red Chilli Enchiladas

*These enchiladas are served stacked, in the traditional New Mexican style,
but you can always roll them up with the filling if you prefer.*

Serves 4

INGREDIENTS

2-3 tbsp masa harina or 1 corn
tortilla, crushed or crumbled
4 tbsp mild chilli powder, such as
New Mexico
2 tbsp paprika
2 garlic cloves, finely chopped
¼ tsp ground cumin
pinch of ground cinnamon

pinch of ground allspice
pinch of dried oregano
1 tbsp lime juice
1 litre/1¾ pints/4 cups vegetable,
chicken or beef stock, simmering
8 flour tortillas
about 450 g/1 lb cooked chicken or
pork, cut into pieces
80 g/3 oz grated cheese

1 tbsp extra-virgin olive oil
4-6 eggs

TO SERVE:
½ onion, finely chopped
1 tbsp finely chopped fresh coriander
(cilantro)
salsa of your choice

1 Mix the masa harina with the chilli powder, paprika, garlic, cumin, cinnamon, allspice, oregano and enough water to make a thin paste. Process in a blender or food processor until smooth.

2 Stir the paste into the simmering stock, reduce the heat and cook until it thickens slightly, then remove the sauce from the heat and stir in the lime juice.

3 Dip the tortillas into the warm sauce. Cover one tortilla with some of the cooked meat. Top with a second dipped tortilla and more meat filling.

Make 3 more towers in this way, then transfer to an ovenproof dish.

4 Pour the remaining sauce over the tortillas, then sprinkle with the grated cheese. Bake in a preheated oven at 180°C/ 350°F/ Gas Mark 4 for 15-20 minutes or until the cheese has melted.

5 Meanwhile, heat the olive oil in a non-stick frying pan (skillet) and cook the eggs until the whites are set and the yolks are still soft.

6 To serve the enchiladas, top each with a fried egg. Serve with the onion mixed with fresh coriander (cilantro) and salsa.

Chicken Tortilla Flutes with Guacamole

These crisply fried, rolled tortillas are known as flauta, *meaning 'flutes' in Mexican, because of their delicate, long shape.*

Serves 4

INGREDIENTS

8 corn tortillas
350 g/12 oz cooked chicken, diced
1 tsp mild chilli powder
1 onion, chopped

1–2 tbsp crème fraîche
vegetable oil, for frying
2 tbsp finely chopped fresh coriander
(cilantro)

1 quantity of Guacamole
(see page 4)
salsa of your choice
salt

1 Heat the tortillas in an ungreased non-stick frying pan (skillet) in a stack, alternating the top and bottom tortillas so that all of the tortillas warm evenly. Wrap in kitchen foil or a clean tea towel (dish cloth) to keep warm

2 Place the chicken in a bowl with the chilli powder, half the onion, half the coriander (cilantro) and salt to taste. Add enough crème fraîche to hold the mixture together.

3 Arrange 2 corn tortillas on the work surface so that they are overlapping, then spoon some of the filling along the centre. Roll up very tightly and secure in place with a toothpick or two. Repeat with the remaining tortillas and filling.

4 Heat oil in a deep frying pan (skillet) until hot and fry the rolls until golden and crisp. Carefully remove from the oil and drain on paper towels.

5 Serve immediately, garnishing with the guacamole, salsa, diced tomato and the remaining onion and fresh coriander (cilantro).

VARIATION

Replace the chicken with seafood, such as cooked prawns (shrimp) or crab meat, and serve the rolls with lemon wedges.

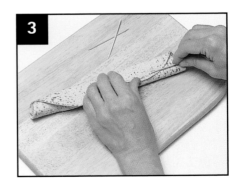

Pork Quesadilla
with Pinto Beans

These melt-in-the-mouth tortilla parcels have a lovely pork, bean and melted cheese filling. Any leftover cooked meat may be used instead of the Carnitas.

Serves 4

INGREDIENTS

1 quantity of Carnitas (see page 42) or about 100 g/3½ oz cooked pork strips per person
1 ripe tomato, deseeded and diced
½ onion, chopped
3 tbsp chopped fresh coriander (cilantro)
4 large flour tortillas

350 g/12 oz grated or thinly sliced cheese, such as mozzarella or gouda
about 375 g/13½ oz cooked drained pinto beans
hot salsa of your choice or bottled hot sauce, to taste

pickled jalapeño chillies, cut into thin rings, to taste
vegetable oil, for frying

TO SERVE:
pickled chillies
mixed salad

1 Heat the Carnitas in a pan and keep hot over a low heat.

2 Combine the tomato, onion and coriander (cilantro) in a bowl and set aside.

3 Heat a tortilla in an ungreased non-stick frying pan (skillet). Sprinkle the tortilla with cheese, then top with some of the meat, beans and reserved tomato mixture. Add salsa and pickled jalapeños to taste. Fold over the sides to make a parcel.

4 Heat the parcels gently on each side in the frying pan (skillet), adding a few drops of oil to keep it all supple and succulent, until the tortilla is golden and the cheese inside has melted. Keep warm. Repeat with the remaining tortillas and filling.

5 Transfer the quesadillas to a plate and serve at once, with pickled chillies and salad.

Green Chilli & Chicken Chilaquiles

Easy to put together, this dish makes a perfect mid-week supper.
Use tortilla chips instead of baking the tortillas, if you prefer.

Serves 4–6

INGREDIENTS

12 stale tortillas, cut into strips
1 tbsp vegetable oil
1 small cooked chicken, meat
  removed from the bones and cut
  into bite-sized pieces
Salsa
3 tbsp chopped fresh coriander
  (cilantro)
1 tsp finely chopped fresh oregano
  or thyme

4 garlic cloves, finely chopped
¼ tsp ground cumin
350 g/12 oz grated cheese, such
  as Cheddar, manchego or
  mozzarella
450 ml/16 fl oz/2 cups chicken
  stock
about 115 g/4 oz/1⅓ cups freshly
  grated Parmesan cheese

TO SERVE:
350 ml/12 fl oz/1½ cups crème
  fraîche or soured cream
3–5 spring onions (scallions), thinly
  sliced
pickled chillies

1 Place the tortilla strips in a roasting tin (pan), toss with the oil and bake in a preheated oven at 190°C/375°F/Gas Mark 5 for about 30 minutes until they are crisp and golden.

2 Arrange the chicken in a 23 x 33 cm/9 x 13 inch casserole, then sprinkle with half the salsa, coriander (cilantro), oregano, garlic, cumin and some of the soft

cheese. Repeat these layers and top with the tortilla strips.

3 Pour the stock over the top, then sprinkle with the remaining cheeses.

4 Bake in a preheated oven at 190°C/375°F/Gas Mark 5 for about 30 minutes until heated through and the cheese is lightly golden in areas.

5 Serve garnished with the crème fraîche, sliced spring onions (scallions) and pickled chillies to taste.

VARIATION

For a vegetarian Mexicana filling, add diced sautéed tofu and sweetcorn kernels in place of the cooked chicken.

Burritos of Lamb & Black Beans

Stir-fried marinated lamb strips are paired with earthy black beans in these tasty burritos.

Serves 4

INGREDIENTS

650 g/1 lb 5 oz lean lamb
3 garlic cloves, finely chopped
juice of ½ lime
½ tsp mild chilli powder
½ tsp ground cumin

large pinch of dried oregano leaves, crushed
1–2 tbsp extra-virgin olive oil
400 g/14 oz cooked black beans, seasoned with a little cumin, salt and pepper

4 large flour tortillas
2–3 tbsp chopped fresh coriander (cilantro)
salsa
salt and pepper

1 Slice the lamb into thin strips, then combine with the garlic, lime juice, chilli powder, cumin, oregano and olive oil. Season with salt and pepper. Leave to marinate in the refrigerator for 4 hours.

2 Warm the black beans with a little water in a pan.

3 Heat the tortillas in an ungreased non-stick frying pan (skillet), sprinkling them with a few drops of water as they heat; wrap the tortillas in a clean tea towel (dish cloth) as you work to keep them warm. Alternatively, heat through in a stack in the pan, alternating the top and bottom tortillas so that they warm evenly. Wrap to keep warm.

4 Stir-fry the lamb in a heavy-based non-stick frying pan over high heat until browned on all sides. Remove from the heat.

5 Spoon some of the beans and browned meat into a tortilla, sprinkle with coriander (cilantro), then dab with salsa and roll up. Repeat with the remaining tortillas and serve at once.

VARIATION

Add a spoonful or two of cooked rice to each burrito.

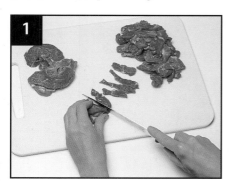

Mexican Refried Beans 'With Everything'

These are refried beans fit for a fiesta, rich with everything – bacon, fried onions, tomatoes, even a bit of beer! As delicious as it sounds!

Serves 4

INGREDIENTS

1–2 tbsp vegetable oil
1–1½ large onions, chopped
125 g/4½ oz bacon lardons or bacon cut into small pieces
3–4 garlic cloves, finely chopped
about 1 tsp ground cumin
½ tsp mild chilli powder

400 g/14 oz can tomatoes, diced and drained, reserving about 150–175 ml/5–6 fl oz/⅗–¾ cup of their juices
400 g/14 oz can refried beans, broken up into pieces
100 ml/3½ fl oz/scant ½ cup beer

400 g/14 oz can pinto beans, drained
salt and pepper

TO SERVE:
warmed flour tortillas
soured cream
sliced pickled chillies

1 Heat the oil in a frying pan (skillet). Add the onion and bacon and fry for about 5 minutes until they are just turning brown. Stir in the garlic, cumin and chilli powder and continue to cook for a minute. Add the tomatoes and cook over a medium-high heat until the liquid has evaporated.

2 Add the refried beans and mash lightly in the pan with the tomato mixture, adding beer as needed to thin out the beans and make them smoother. Lower the heat and cook, stirring, until the mixture is smooth and creamy.

3 Add the pinto beans and stir well to combine; if the mixture is too thick, add a little of the reserved tomato juice. Adjust the spicing to taste. Season with salt and pepper and serve with warmed tortillas, soured cream and sliced chillies.

VARIATION

Top the dish with grated cheese, then pop under a preheated grill (broiler) to melt and sizzle. Serve at once. This makes a luscious filling for warm flour tortillas.

Spicy Fragrant Black Bean Chilli

Black beans are fragrant and flavourful; enjoy this chillied bean stew Mexican style with soft tortillas, or Californian style in a bowl with crisp tortillas chips crumbled in.

Serves 4

INGREDIENTS

400 g/14 oz dried black beans
2 tbsp olive oil
1 onion, chopped
5 garlic cloves, coarsely chopped
2 slices bacon, diced (optional)

½–1 tsp ground cumin
½–1 tsp mild red chilli powder
1 red (bell) pepper, diced
1 carrot, diced
400 g/14 oz fresh tomatoes, diced, or

chopped canned
1 bunch fresh coriander (cilantro),
  coarsely chopped
salt and pepper

1 Soak the beans overnight, then drain. Put in a pan, cover with water and bring to the boil. Boil for 10 minutes, then reduce the heat and simmer for about 1½ hours until tender. Drain well, reserving 225 ml/8 fl oz/1 cup of the cooking liquid.

2 Heat the oil in a frying pan (skillet). Add the onion and garlic and fry for 2 minutes, stirring. Stir in the bacon, if using, and cook, stirring occasionally, until the bacon is cooked and the onion is soften.

3 Stir in the cumin and red chilli powder and continue to cook for a moment or two. Add the red (bell) pepper, carrot and tomatoes. Cook over a medium heat for about 5 minutes.

4 Add half the coriander (cilantro) and the beans and their reserved liquid. Season with salt and pepper. Simmer for 30–45 minutes or until very flavourful and thickened.

5 Stir through the remaining coriander (cilantro), adjust the seasoning and serve at once.

COOK'S TIP

You can use canned beans, if wished: drain and use 225 ml/ 8 fl oz/1 cup water for the liquid added in Step 4.

Jalisco-style Eggs

This hearty breakfast dish from Jalisco is a classic Mexican way of serving eggs – a feast of flavours!

Serves 4

INGREDIENTS

4 corn tortillas
1 avocado
lime or lemon juice, for tossing
175 g/6 oz chorizo sausage, sliced or diced

2 tbsp butter or water, for cooking
4 eggs
4 tbsp feta or Wensleydale cheese, crumbled
salsa of your choice

1 tbsp chopped fresh coriander (cilantro)
1 tbsp finely chopped spring onions (scallions)

1 Heat the tortillas in an ungreased non-stick frying pan (skillet), sprinkling them with a few drops of water as they heat; wrap the tortillas in a clean tea towel (dish cloth) as you work to keep them warm. Alternatively, heat through in a stack in the pan, alternating the top and bottom tortillas so that they warm evenly. Wrap to keep warm.

2 Cut the avocado in half around the stone (pit). Twist apart, then remove the stone (pit) with a knife. Carefully peel off the skin, dice the flesh and toss in lime or lemon juice to prevent discoloration.

3 Brown the chorizo sausage in a pan, then arrange on each warmed tortilla. Keep warm.

4 Meanwhile, heat the butter or water in the non-stick frying pan (skillet), break in an egg and cook until the white is set but the yolk still soft. Remove from the pan and place on top of one tortilla. Keep warm.

5 Cook the remaining eggs in the same way, adding to the tortillas.

6 Arrange the avocado, cheese and a spoonful of salsa on each tortilla. Add the fresh coriander (cilantro) and spring onions (scallions) and serve.

Migas

A wonderful brunch or late-night supper dish, this is made by scrambling egg with chillies, tomatoes and crisp tortilla chips.

Serves 4

INGREDIENTS

2 tbsp butter
6 garlic cloves, finely chopped
1 fresh green chilli, such as jalapeño
   or serrano, deseeded and diced
1½ tsp ground cumin

6 ripe tomatoes, coarsely chopped
8 eggs, lightly beaten
8–10 corn tortillas, cut into strips and
   fried until crisp, or an equal amount
   of not too salty tortilla chips

4 tbsp chopped fresh coriander
   (cilantro)
3–4 spring onions (scallions), thinly
   sliced
mild chilli powder, to garnish

1 Melt half the butter in a pan. Add the garlic and chilli and cook until softened, but not browned. Add the cumin and cook for 30 seconds, stirring, then add the tomatoes and cook over a medium heat for a further 3–4 minutes, or until the tomato juices have evaporated. Remove from the pan and set aside.

2 Melt the remaining butter in a frying pan (skillet) over a low heat and pour in the beaten eggs. Cook, stirring, until the eggs begin to set.

3 Add the reserved chilli tomato mixture, stirring gently to mix into the eggs.

4 Carefully add the tortilla strips or chips and continue cooking, stirring once or twice, until the eggs are the consistency you wish. The tortillas should be pliable and chewy.

5 Transfer to a serving plate and surround with the fresh coriander (cilantro) and spring onions. Garnish with a sprinkling of mild chilli powder and serve.

COOK'S TIP

Serve the migas with soured cream or crème fraîche on top, to melt seductively into the spicy eggs.

VARIATION

Add browned minced (ground) beef or pork to the softly scrambling egg mixture at Step 3. A bunch of cooked, chopped, spinach or chard can be stirred in as well, to add fresh colour.

Eggs Oaxaca Style

Cooking eggs in a flat omelette, then cutting them into strips and simmering them in a spicy sauce makes an unusual dish for brunch or dinner.

Serves 4

INGREDIENTS

1 kg/2 lb 4 oz ripe tomatoes
about 12 small button onions, halved
8 garlic cloves, whole and unpeeled
2 fresh mild green chillies
pinch of ground cumin

pinch of dried oregano,
pinch of sugar, if needed
2–3 tsp vegetable oil
8 eggs, lightly beaten
1–2 tbsp tomato purée (paste)

salt and pepper
1–2 tbsp chopped fresh coriander
(cilantro), to garnish

1 Heat an ungreased heavy-based frying pan (skillet), add the tomatoes and char lightly, turning them once or twice. Allow to cool.

2 Meanwhile lightly char the onions, garlic and chillies in the pan. Allow to cool slightly.

3 Cut the cooled tomatoes into pieces and place in a blender or food processor, with their charred skins. Remove the stems and seeds from the chillies, then peel and chop. Remove the skins from the garlic, then chop. Roughly chop the onions. Add the chillies, garlic and onions to the tomatoes.

4 Process to make a rough purée, then add the cumin and oregano. Season with salt and pepper to taste, and add sugar if needed.

5 Heat the oil in a non-stick frying pan (skillet), add a ladleful of egg and cook to make a thin omelette. Continue to make omelettes, stacking them on a plate as they are cooked. Slice into noodle-like ribbons.

6 Bring the sauce to the boil, adjust the seasoning, adding tomato purée (paste) to taste. Add the omelette strips, warm through and serve at once, garnished with a sprinkling of fresh coriander (cilantro).

Eggs with Refried Beans

In the Yucatan, this classic dish would be sandwiched between two crisp tortillas,
but layering it all on top of one tortilla looks much more festive.

Serves 4

INGREDIENTS

400 g/14 oz tomatoes, skinned and
  chopped
1 onion, chopped
1 garlic clove, finely chopped
½ fresh green chilli, such as jalapeño
  or serrano, deseeded and chopped
¼ tsp ground cumin
2 tbsp extra-virgin olive oil
1 plantain, peeled and diced

1 tbsp butter
4 corn tortillas, warmed or fried
  crisply into a tostada
about 400 g/14 oz can refried beans,
  warmed with 2 tbsp of water
2 tbsp water or butter
8 eggs
1 red (bell) pepper, grilled (broiled),
  peeled, deseeded and cut into strips

3–4 tbsp cooked green peas, at room
  temperature
4–6 tbsp diced cooked or smoked
  ham
50–75 g/2–3 oz crumbled feta cheese
3 spring onions (scallions), thinly
  sliced
salt and pepper

1 Process the tomatoes in a blender or food processor with the onion, garlic, chilli, cumin, salt and pepper to a purée.

2 Heat the oil in a heavy-based frying pan (skillet), then ladle in a little of the sauce and cook until it reduces in volume and becomes almost paste-like. Continue adding and reducing the sauce in this way. Keep warm.

3 Brown the plantain in the butter in a heavy-based non-stick frying pan (skillet). Remove and set aside. Spread the tortillas with the refried beans and keep warm in a low oven.

4 Heat the water or butter in the frying pan (skillet), break in an egg and cook until the white is set but the yolk still soft. Remove from the pan and place on top of one tortilla. Cook the remaining eggs in the same way, adding to the tortillas.

5 To serve, spoon the warm sauce around the eggs on each tortilla. Sprinkle over the diced plantain, (bell) pepper, peas, ham, feta cheese and spring onions (scallions). Season with salt and pepper to taste and serve immediately.

Spicy Grilled (Broiled) Salmon

*The woody smoked flavours of the chipotle chilli are delicious brushed
on to salmon for grilling (broiling).*

Serves 4

INGREDIENTS

4 salmon steaks, about
175–225 g/6–8 oz each
lime slices, to garnish

MARINADE:
4 garlic cloves
2 tbsp extra-virgin olive oil
pinch of ground allspice

pinch of ground cinnamon
juice of 2 limes
1–2 tsp marinade from canned
chipotle chillies or bottled chipotle
chilli salsa
¼ tsp ground cumin
pinch of sugar
salt and pepper

TO SERVE:
tomato wedges
3 spring onions (scallions) finely
chopped
shredded lettuce

1 To make the marinade, finely chop the garlic and place in a bowl with the olive oil, allspice, cinnamon, lime juice, chipotle marinade, cumin and sugar. Add salt and pepper and stir to combine.

2 Coat the salmon with the garlic mixture, then place in a non-metallic dish. Leave to marinate for at least an hour or overnight in the refrigerator.

3 Transfer to a grill (broiler) pan and cook under a preheated grill (broiler) for 3–4 minutes on each side. Alternatively, cook the salmon over hot coals on a barbecue (grill) until cooked through.

4 To serve, mix the tomato wedges with the spring onions (scallions). Place the salmon on individual plates and arrange the tomato salad and

shredded lettuce alongside. Garnish with lime slices and serve immediately.

VARIATION

*The marinade
also goes well with fresh tuna
steaks.*

Carnitas

*In this classic Mexican dish, pieces of pork are first simmered to make
them meltingly tender, then browned until irresistibly crisp.*

Serves 4–6

INGREDIENTS

1 kg/2 lb 4 oz pork, such as
  lean belly
1 onion, chopped
1 whole garlic bulb, cut in half
½ tsp ground cumin
2 meat stock cubes

2 bay leaves
vegetable oil, for frying
salt and pepper
fresh chilli strips, to garnish

TO SERVE:
cooked rice
refried beans
salsa of your choice

1 Place the pork in a heavy-based pan with the onion, garlic, cumin, stock cubes and bay leaves. Add water to cover. Bring to the boil, then reduce the heat to very low. Skim off the foam and scum that has formed on the surface of the liquid.

2 Continue to cook very gently for about 2 hours or until the meat is tender. Remove from the heat and leave the meat to cool in the liquid.

3 Remove the meat from the pan with a slotted spoon. Cut off any rind (roast separately to make crackling). Cut the meat into bite-sized pieces and sprinkle with salt and pepper. Reserve 300 ml/10 fl oz/1¼ cups of the cooking liquid.

4 Brown the meat in a heavy-based frying pan (skillet) for about 15 minutes, to cook out the fat. Add the reserved meat cooking liquid and allow to reduce down. Continue to cook the meat for 15 minutes, covering the pan to avoid splattering. Turn the meat every now and again.

5 Transfer the meat to a serving dish, garnish with chilli strips and serve with rice, refried beans and salsa.

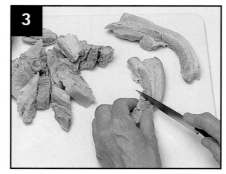

Simmered Stew of Meat, Chicken, Vegetables & Fruit

A big pot of cocido *is warming on a cold day, great for a family meal. Serve with a selection of several salsas, a stack of corn tortillas and a bowl of rice.*

Serves 6–8

INGREDIENTS

900 g/2 lb boneless pork, either in one joint or in pieces
2 bay leaves
1 onion, chopped
8 garlic cloves, finely chopped
2 tbsp chopped fresh coriander (cilantro)
1 carrot, thinly sliced
2 celery sticks, diced

2 chicken stock cubes
½ chicken, cut into portions
4–5 ripe tomatoes, diced
½ tsp mild chilli powder
grated rind of ¼ orange
¼ tsp ground cumin
juice of 3 oranges
1 courgette (zucchini), cut into bite-sized pieces

¼ cabbage, thinly sliced and blanched
1 apple, cut into bite-sized pieces
about 10 prunes, stoned (pitted)
¼ tsp ground cinnamon
pinch of dried ginger
2 hard chorizo sausages, about 350 g/12 oz in total, cut into bite-sized pieces
salt and pepper

1 Combine the pork, bay leaves, onion, garlic, coriander (cilantro), carrot and celery in a large pan and fill with cold water. Bring to the boil, skim off the scum on the surface. Reduce heat and simmer gently for an hour.

2 Add the stock cubes to the pan, along with the chicken, tomatoes, chilli powder, orange rind and cumin. Continue to cook for a further 45 minutes or until the chicken is tender. Spoon off the fat that forms on the top of the liquid.

3 Add the orange juice, courgette (zucchini), cabbage, apple, prunes, cinnamon, ginger and chorizo. Continue to simmer for a further 20 minutes or until the courgette (zucchini) is soft and tender and the chorizo cooked through.

4 Season the stew with salt and pepper to taste. Serve immediately with rice, tortillas and salsa.

Chicken Breasts in Green Salsa with Soured Cream

Chicken breasts bathed in a fragrant sauce make a delicate dish, perfect for dinner parties. Serve with rice to complete the meal.

Serves 4

INGREDIENTS

4 chicken breast fillets
flour, for dredging
2–3 tbsp butter or combination
  butter and oil
450 g/1 lb mild green salsa or
  puréed tomatillos
225 ml/8 fl oz /1 cup
  chicken stock

1–2 garlic cloves, finely chopped
3–5 tbsp chopped fresh coriander
  (cilantro)
½ fresh green chilli, deseeded and
  chopped
½ tsp ground cumin
salt and pepper

TO SERVE:
225 ml/8 fl oz/1 cup soured cream
several leaves cos (romaine) lettuce,
  shredded
3–5 spring onions (scallions), thinly
  sliced
coarsely chopped fresh coriander
  (cilantro)

1 Sprinkle the chicken with salt and pepper, then dredge in flour. Shake off the excess.

2 Melt the butter in a frying pan (skillet), add the chicken and cook over a medium-high heat, turning once, until they are golden but not cooked through – they will continue to cook slightly in the sauce. Remove from pan and set aside.

3 Place the salsa, chicken stock, garlic, coriander (cilantro), chilli and cumin in a pan and bring to the boil. Reduce the heat to a low simmer. Add the chicken breasts to the sauce, spooning the sauce over the chicken. Continue to cook until the chicken is cooked through.

4 Remove the chicken from the pan and season with salt and pepper to taste. Serve with the soured cream, shredded lettuce, sliced spring onions (scallions) and chopped fresh coriander leaves.

This is a Parragon Book
First published in 2003

Parragon
Queen Street House
4 Queen Street, Bath, BA1 1HE, UK

Copyright © Parragon 2003

All recipes and photography compiled from material
created by 'Haldane Mason', and 'The Foundry'.

Cover design by Shelley Doyle.

ISBN: 1-40540-827-8

Printed in China

NOTE

This book uses imperial and metric measurements. Follow the same units
of measurement throughout; do not mix imperial and metric. All spoon
measurements are level; teaspoons are assumed to be 5 ml and
tablespoons are assumed to be 15 ml. Unless otherwise stated, milk is
assumed to be whole milk, eggs and individual vegetables such as
potatoes are medium, and pepper is freshly ground black pepper.

The times given for each recipe are an approximate guide only because
the preparation times may differ according to the techniques used by
different people and the cooking times may vary as a result of the type of
oven used.

Recipes using raw or very lightly cooked eggs should be avoided by
infants, the elderly, pregnant women, convalescents and anyone suffering
from an illness.